DIESELS IN THE
NORTH ~ EAST

Plate 1: Class 37, No. 37006 moves around the sidings at Easington Colliery on 9th January 1981, prior to heading a waste train destined for Seaham Harbour.

David H. Allen

Plate 2: Class 55 'Deltic', No. 55016 *Gordon Highlander* pauses at Durham, with the 09.50 Edinburgh to Plymouth train, on 10th October 1981.

David H. Allen

DIESELS
in the
NORTH ~ EAST

David H. Allen

Oxford Publishing Company

Typesetting by:
Aquarius Typesetting Services, New Milton, Hants.

Printed in Great Britain by:
Biddles Ltd., Guildford, Surrey.

Published by:
Oxford Publishing Co.
Link House
West Street
POOLE, Dorset

Introduction

The North-East was the birthplace of the locomotive-hauled railway. The first routes were built to carry coal and, to the present day, coal provides an important, if not declining revenue for the railways.

In railway terms, the North-East, defined in this instance as Northumberland, Durham, Tyne & Wear and Cleveland, is like a corridor, bounded between the Pennines and the North Sea. With few exceptions, the main emphasis is on north to south movements, which coincides with the East Coast Main Line (ECML). At times during its history, the ECML has been the poor relation to the West Coast equivalent. Beeching, in his report, envisaged the truncation of the ECML north of Newcastle! In the 1970s, the West Coast Main Line was electrified. However, the introduction of the HST has more than restored the balance for the ECML. But what of the future? Electrification, or rationalization based on Serpell?

The only important east-west route is along the Tyne Valley. Low investment, combined with the difficult nature of the terrain in the west, have combined to produce poor line speeds. In the two hours it takes to reach Carlisle from Newcastle, a traveller could be speeding near Peterborough on the main line! Links with Scotland and the rest of England are considered more important than those with our West Coast friends.

The Durham Coast line is a shadow of its former self, with the disappearance of the regular expresses to Liverpool and East Anglia, and just one early morning departure for King's Cross. On the 13 mile stretch between Seaham and Hartlepool, there is no intermediate station.

The freight business has suffered from a reliance on the traditional industries, including coal, steel and shipbuilding, which are all in decline. Movements out of the coalfield have gradually moved eastwards, as the coal has been exhausted. Modern workings are largely confined to operations under the North Sea, for example, Easington and Seaham. With the run-down of steel-making at Hartlepool and Skinningrove, and the complete closure at Consett, the industry has become concentrated on Teesside. This, combined with the massive chemical and petroleum industry around the River Tees, emphasises the increasing importance of Teesside, in relative terms, as a railway centre.

North of the Tyne, British Rail has only one passenger route, this being the ECML. The extensive ex-Blyth & Tyne network, centred around Bedlington, is almost exclusively concerned with coal movements, an exception being alumina from North Blyth to the Lynemouth Smelter.

Many of the freight routes are important diversionary routes for the ECML. In fact, with the exception of the stretch between Benton and Heaton, it is possible to divert ECML services south of Morpeth. This assumes that the slow lines can be used when there are four tracks. There are even two bridges across the Tyne!

To meet changing consumer requirements and to adapt to the very strong competition from road transport, the railways have undergone considerable modification over recent years. The photographs contributed by Ian Carr illustrate some of the more interesting scenes that can no longer be seen. These include green liveried 'Deltics', semaphore signals on the ECML and Class 29s on delivery to the Scottish Region. However, one has only got to go back a few years to witness the slow tide of change. Even as I write, the last freight train has just run to Consett. The 'Deltics' have been completely replaced by HSTs, and although much lamented by the enthusiast, the latter have revitalized the Inter-City passenger scene. As recently as April 1982, the well-known Penshaw signal box was closed as the result of a small power scheme. Even the massive Tyne Yard, barely 20 years old, seems ready for closure. Much of the recent material is therefore already part of the archives.

In conclusion, I would like to thank all British Rail staff who, knowingly or unknowingly, have helped me in my photographic 'adventure'.

David H. Allen
Durham City

Plate 3: Metro-Cammell two car set, comprising cars E50253 and E56391, forms the 13.10 Hexham to Newcastle train on 31st August 1982, as it approaches Cowans Crossing. The signal box at Cowans Crossing was closed on 27th April 1983 and the semaphore signals were removed the same day.

David H. Allen

Plate 4: The 09.15 Edinburgh to King's Cross train disturbs the freshly fallen snow as it crosses Plawsworth Viaduct, on 11th December 1981. The power cars, Nos. 43175 and 43176, had only recently entered revenue earning service.

David H. Allen

Plate 5: In original two-tone green livery and as yet unnamed, Class 55 'Deltic', No. D9019 drifts through Manors with the 'up' 'Flying Scotsman', on 1st August 1964. Note the attractive headboard and the full rake of maroon Mk. I passenger stock.

Ian S. Carr

Plate 6: Class 45/1 'Peak' No. 45135 *3rd Carabinier* passes Hett Mill with the 12.05 (SuO) Newcastle to Liverpool train, on 14th March 1982. The crossing gates have since been replaced by barriers and the box has been closed. Hett Mill was one of the last gated crossings on the East Coast Main Line.

David H. Allen

Plate 7: Shortly after leaving Darlington, Class 45/1 'Peak', No. 45148 heads the 10.40 (SuO) Liverpool to Newcastle train while passing near to Coatham Mundeville, on 24th May 1981.

David H. Allen

Plate 8: Class 55 'Deltic', No. 55003 *Meld* speeds south through Plawsworth, with the 14.53 (SuO) Newcastle to Doncaster train, on 6th July 1980. This train only ran during the summer, with the locomotive and stock working north on the 08.40 service from King's Cross.

David H. Allen

Plate 9: Class 55 'Deltic', No. 55013 *The Black Watch* heads north after pausing at Durham with the 05.50 King's Cross to Aberdeen train, on 17th August 1981. This train remains locomotive-hauled, but only works north of York.

David H. Allen

Plate 10: The late-running diesel multiple unit, forming the 17.10 Durham to Newcastle service, pulls out of Chester-le-Street Station, just as Class 40, No. 40004 enters with the 17.18 Newcastle to Liverpool train, on 9th September 1982. Following the withdrawal of two local southbound services, two Inter-City trains now stop here.

David H. Allen

Plate 11: Class 45 'Peak', No. 45076 takes water at Newcastle, prior to departing with the 13.22 service for Liverpool, on 18th December 1982.

Craig Oliphant

Plate 12:   On the northerly approach to Darlington, Class 47/4, No. 47441 passes Haughton, with the 15.30 Newcastle to Liverpool service, on 18th October 1980.

David H. Allen

Plate 13:   Class 47/4, No. 47430 heads the 07.05 Newcastle to Edinburgh train through Acklington, on 25th July 1981. This train is also conveying sleeping cars, originally off the 01.00 King's Cross to Newcastle service. This rural station still retains much of its grandeur!

David H. Allen

Plate 14: Class 45 'Peak', No. D56 *The Bedfordshire and Hertfordshire Regiment (T. A.)* (since renumbered 45137) prepares to enter Heaton sidings, on 15th June 1963, with empty carriage stock. The V3 class steam locomotive, No. 67651 is preparing for an empty stock movement into Newcastle.

Ian S. Carr

Plate 15: The Hawker Siddeley/Brush prototype diesel locomotive *Kestrel*, in sparkling yellow and chocolate livery, waits at Heaton Carriage Sheds on 28th October 1969, with empty stock for the 16.45 Newcastle to King's Cross train. Note the correct use of the train describer, even for the short run into Newcastle Central Station.

Ian S.Carr

Plate 18: Class 37, No. 37052 crosses the imposing viaduct at Chester-le-Street, while heading the 14.03 (SO) Newcastle to Clifton carriage sidings, on 2nd July 1983. The locomotive and stock had earlier worked the 10.35 (SO) Scarborough to Newcastle train. The locomotive was still immaculate, after being specially prepared at Stratford to work the last scheduled Class 37 service, working from Liverpool Street to King's Lynn.

David H. Allen

Plate 16 (above left): An enthusiast savours Class 55 'Deltic', No. 55015 *Tulyar*, gleaming under the roof at Bank Top Station, prior to departure with the 07.22 Plymouth to Edinburgh train, on 14th April 1981.

David H. Allen

Plate 17 (below left): Class 55 'Deltic', No. 55010 *The King's Own Scottish Borderer* passes through Heaton, with the 09.10 Dundee to King's Cross train, on 10th August 1981. The nearside nameplate is missing from the locomotive.

David H. Allen

Just Memories

Plate 19: Class 24/1, No. D5104 (later renumbered 24104) passes Three Horse Shoes signal box, on 26th August 1966, with a train of iron-ore empties from Consett to Tyne Dock. Soon afterwards the route between Washington and Pontop Crossing closed. This locomotive was one of the batch built at the British Railways workshops at Darlington.

Ian S. Carr

Plate 20: For the last operative years of the Consett Steelworks, the iron ore was imported via the Redcar ore terminal. In this instance, a train of empties is hauled by Class 37 locomotives, Nos. 37173 and 37070, working in multiple past Guisborough Junction, on 10th June 1980. Before its destruction by fire the previous weekend, Guisborough Junction could boast the largest mechanical signal box in the north-east.

David H. Allen

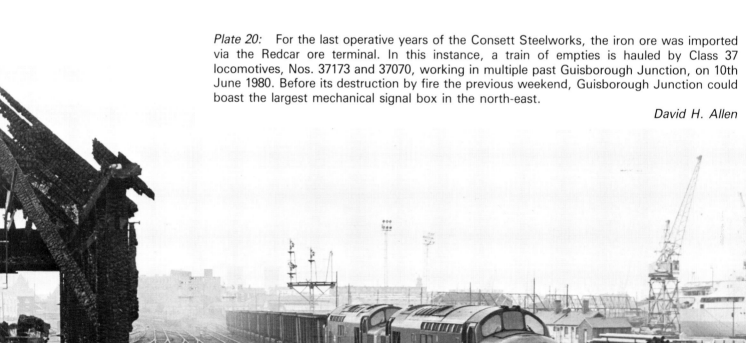

Plate 21: The regular passenger service on the Deerness Valley route was suspended in 1951. However, heading a day excursion from Ushaw Moor to Redcar, Class 25/0, No. D5171 (later renumbered 25021) comes off the branch at Deerness Valley Junction, on 27th July 1963.

Ian S. Carr

Plate 22: A Sunderland to Durham parcels train passes through Pallion, on 23rd April 1963, headed by Class 24/1, No. D5110 (later renumbered 24110). The route of this train was via Penshaw and Auckland Junction. Pallion is now the end of a short branch from Hendon.

Ian S. Carr

Plate 23: The passenger service to Crook was discontinued in 1965. Passing under the lower quadrant gantry to the south of Bishop Auckland Station, a green-liveried three car Metro-Cammell diesel multiple unit heads a train from Darlington, on 8th April 1964.

Ian S. Carr

Plate 24: A Derby lightweight diesel multiple unit leaves West Auckland Station, with the 16.15 Bishop Auckland to Barnard Castle train, on 27th February 1962. The route was closed just four months afterwards.

Ian S. Carr

Plate 25: Class 40, No. D222 *Laconia* (since renumbered 40022) draws to a halt in Sunderland, while heading a Newcastle to Liverpool train, which will run via the coast. The station is in the early stages of reconstruction, whilst the carriages are of a pre-nationalization type.

Ian S. Carr

Plate 26: The afternoon service from Bishop Auckland to Durham pauses at Hunwick, not long before the withdrawal of passenger services in May 1964.

Ian S. Carr

Plate 27: A refurbished Class 101 two car diesel multiple unit, composed of cars E51222 and E56380, pauses at Tyne Dock while forming the 12.38 South Shields to Newcastle train, on 28th March 1981. The train is on the short single line section between Harton Junction and South Shields. British Rail services were suspended on 6th June 1981, pending the development of the Tyneside Metro.

David H. Allen

Plate 28: At the time of withdrawal of passenger services on the Riverside branch in 1973, trains were limited to morning and evening periods. Entering Walker on 9th July 1973, is a Derby diesel multiple unit, forming the 16.24 Newcastle to Newcastle (Circle) train. The chairs from the third rail electrification can still be seen.

Ian S. Carr

Plate 29: The South Shields branch joins the coast route at Pelaw. The diesel multiple unit on the left has just come off the branch with the 14.08 ex-South Shields train, whereas the other diesel multiple unit is forming the 14.12 train from Sunderland to Newcastle. The late 1950s signal box has since been abolished, and the area is now controlled by Gateshead West.

David H. Allen

Plate 30: A Newcastle to Middlesbrough train climbs out of Sunderland towards Fawcett Street Junction, on 5th April 1964. Engineering work on the coast line required such trains to be diverted via Sedgefield. This connection has since been closed, but the route to Hendon, which is shown in the foreground, remains open to freight traffic.

Ian S. Carr

Tyne Valley

Plate 32 (above right): Passing under the framework upon which Hexham signal box stands, the 09.42 Carlisle to Newcastle train wends its way along the Tyne Valley. These 'over the track' signal boxes were once quite common in the north-east.

David H. Allen

Plate 33 (below right): The 1981/2 timetable saw the introduction of a daily locomotive-hauled passenger service along the Tyne Valley, which is essentially just an extension of an Edinburgh to Newcastle stopping service. Class 46 'Peak', No. 46045 heads the 15.53 Carlisle to Edinburgh train through Greenhead, on 30th July 1981.

David H. Allen

Plate 31: Haltwhistle, until recently the junction for the Alston branch, still has the charm of an old rural junction. A blue-liveried Class 101 two car diesel multiple unit composed of cars E51213 and E56380, pauses with the 10.42 Carlisle to Newcastle train, on 2nd September 1981.

David H. Allen

Plate 35: Class 101 two car
diesel multiple unit, composed of
cars E56398 and E50221, draws
out of Wylam with the 07.50
Carlisle to Newcastle train, on
16th May 1982.

David H. Allen

Plate 34: Denton Village is a
delightful little crossing box to
the west of Haltwhistle. On 2nd
September 1981, approaching
the crossing, is the 11.35 Carlisle
Yard to Tyne Yard service
headed by Class 37, No. 37219.
The signal in the foreground is
wooden, complete with finial.

David H. Allen

Plate 36: Class 37, No. 37198, passes Bardon Mill signal box with the 11.35 Carlisle Yard to Tyne Yard, on 30th July 1981.

David H. Allen

Plate 37: Class 46 'Peak', No. 46026 *Leicestershire and Derbyshire Yeomanry* approaches Prudhoe, with the 15.53 Carlisle to Newcastle train. At the time, this train was frequently hauled by a 'Deltic' locomotive. The tall signal box is partly obscured by the footbridge.

David H. Allen

Plate 38 (above): As a result of a derailment on the East Coast Main Line on 5th January 1982, all 'up' trains were diverted via Leamside for 36 hours. On 6th January, the 11.21 Newcastle to Liverpool train passes through Shincliffe, hauled by Class 47/0 No. 47051. In the background are the remains of the station, which closed in 1941.

David H. Allen

Plate 39 (above right): Another casualty of the same derailment was the afternoon Speedlink service for Dagenham. It is seen south of Whitwell, hauled by Class 40, No. 40060.

David H. Allen

Plate 40 (below right): Also, on 6th January 1982, an unidentified High Speed Train service, led by power car No. 43162, moves southwards, with caution, on the approaches to Bowburn.

David H. Allen

Plate 41: Class 31/1, No. 31290 shunts in the yard outside the BREL Shildon Wagon Works, prior to departing with a midday working to Tees Yard, on 10th February 1983.

David H. Allen

Plate 42: Sandwiched between two snowploughs, and displaying the snow and ice accumulated during the sub-zero conditions of the previous night, Class 37, No. 37030 idles outside the stabling point at Tyne Yard, on 7th January 1982.

David H. Allen

Plate 43: The 09.27 Durham to Newcastle service passes Birtley Station, on 11th December 1981. The Cravens diesel multiple units arrived after the Great Northern electrification, but are no longer in service in the north-east.

David H. Allen

Plate 44: The 05.50 King's Cross to Aberdeen working speeds through Birtley on 11th December 1981, hauled by Class 55 'Deltic', No. 55017 *The Durham Light Infantry.*

David H. Allen

Teesside . . .

Plate 45:   Having recently emerged from Crewe after an intermediate overhaul, Class 37, No. 37261 leaves the ICI complex at Haverton Hill with the 16.05 Speedlink service for Parkeston Yard, on 23rd August 1982. The line in the distance on the left goes to Port Clarence and Seal Sands.

David H. Allen

Plate 46: A Class 101 two car diesel multiple unit, composed of cars E56387 and E51229, heads out of Stockton and approaches North Shore, on 14th March 1982, with the 10.40 (SuO) Middlesbrough to Newcastle service.

David H. Allen

Plate 47: A Metro-Cammell two car diesel multiple unit, comprising cars E56091 and E50200, passes the BSC Lackenby Works, on 20th March 1982, with the 14.35 Saltburn to Darlington train.

David H. Allen

Plate 48: Stockton Station looks very bare since the overall roof was demolished. Passing through, on 29th March 1981, with the diverted 13.08 Heaton to Manchester (Red Bank) empty vans working, is Class 40, No. 40003.

David H. Allen

Plate 49: Class 45/1 'Peak', No. 45113 heads the 09.55 (SuO) Newcastle to Liverpool service, under the imposing ex-North Eastern Railway gantry at North Shore, on 14th March 1982.

David H. Allen

Plate 50: Class 55 'Deltic' No. 55021 *Argyll & Sutherland Highlander* restarts the diverted 14.57 (SuO) Newcastle to King's Cross service, after a signal check near Eaglescliffe, on 5th July 1981. The platform avoiding lines to the right have since been removed.

David H. Allen

Plate 51: Class 40, No. 40135 crawls into Newcastle, on the 'up' Tynemouth line, with empty stock for the 15.0
Newcastle to Manchester relief train, on Spring Bank Holiday Monday, 1981.

David H. Alle

Plate 52: Minutes before departure, Class 55 'Deltic', No. 55004 *Queen's Own Highlander* noisily prepares to depart from Newcastle with the 13.20 stopping service to Edinburgh, on 19th July 1980. This train was a victim of economy cuts during the following January.

David H. Allen

Plate 53: Class 47/4, No. 47402, since named *Gateshead*, draws out of Newcastle with the 08.05 (SO) Liverpool to Edinburgh train, while Class 40, No. 40182 propels the stock for the 13.10 (SO) departure for Scarborough, on 4th July 1981. The tracks to the right of the Class 40 locomotive have since been removed.

David H. Allen

Plate 54: Complete with a split indicator, Class 45/0 'Peak', No. 45025 passes through Heaton, on 10th January 1981, with a late-running overnight freight train from Millerhill to Tyne Yard.

Les Abram

Plate 55: Propelling a brake tender, Class 17 No. D8592 leaves Trafalgar Yard (Manors) with an 'up' freight train on 1st August 1964. The scene has since drastically changed as the third rail electrification disappeared with the dieselization of the Tynemouth suburban services, and the closure of the Quayside branch saw the end of the overhead catenary.

Ian S. Carr

Plate 56: Class 47/0, No. 47091 stands alongside Newcastle Central Station, with the empty stock that will form the 12.53 relief service to Seaburn. This eleven mile locomotive-hauled trip was in connection with a football match at Sunderland, on 28th November 1981.

David H. Allen

Plate 57: A Class 101 two car diesel multiple unit, composed of cars E56083 and E51252, passes Horden with the 13.15 Newcastle to Middlesbrough train on 4th September 1982. Horden had a passenger station until 1964 but now there is a 13 mile stretch, between Seaham and Hartlepool, without any passenger facilities.

David H. Allen

Plate 58: Eaglescliffe Station boasts the reintroduction of through services from Teesside to London whilst, in the background, the old order is represented by an ageing Metro-Cammell two car diesel multiple unit. It is composed of cars Nos. E56370 and E50157, forming the 11.50 Darlington to Saltburn service, on 14th April 1981.

David H. Allen

Plate 59:   The 15.40 Newcastle to Carlisle service makes an unscheduled stop at Haydon Bridge, on 3rd May 1982. Even though the line is operated by paytrains, the station buildings are remarkably intact.

David H. Allen

Plate 60:   The section of track between Blaydon and Scotswood was closed on 4th October 1982, and all trains now travel over the former freight lines via Norwood Junction. The 09.42 Carlisle to Newcastle train crosses the Tyne, on the now closed section. Maintenance costs of the bridge at Scotswood were a major factor in its closure.

David H. Allen

The Blyth and Tyne

Plate 61 (above): Passing Holywell signal box, close to the site of Backworth Colliery, on 21st June 1982, Class 56, No. 56079 heads the 15.15 Blyth Power-Station to South Hetton empties train.

Paul D. Shannon

Plate 62 (left): Since the withdrawal of passenger services to Newbiggin in November 1964, there is now no regular passenger service on the former Blyth & Tyne network. Standing at the terminus, on 8th August 1964, a green-liveried diesel multiple unit waits to leave with the 16.35 train for Manors, via Seaton Deleval.

Ian S. Carr

Plate 63 (above right): Class 37, No. 37020 heads a train of alumina empties from Lynemouth to North Blyth, past Freemans, on 21st June 1982.

Paul D. Shannon

Plate 64 (below right): Class 37, No. 37065 propels a set of alumina empties under the loading towers at the Alcan terminal at North Blyth, on 3rd September 1982.

David H. Allen

Plate 65: Class 37, No. 37216 prepares to take the route to Marchey's House, on 20th October 1980, with a train of empty hoppers from North Blyth to Lynemouth Colliery.

David H. Allen

Plate 66: Class 37, No. 37060 takes the Morpeth route at Bedlington, on 24th October 1980. Having arrived from the north, this locomotive had to run round its train at Bedlington. The construction of the new Hepscott curve at Morpeth had meant that a similar manoeuvre is no longer necessary at this location.

David H. Allen

Via Leamside

Plate 67: Class 55 'Deltic', No. 55004 *Queen's Own Highlander* heads the 07.36 Plymouth to Edinburgh train through Washington, on 17th October 1981. Damage to an extensive part of the East Coast Main Line south of Ouston Junction, and the subsequent rectification, caused a week-long diversion.

Paul D. Shannon

Plate 68 (above left): The 09.45 (SuO) Newcastle to King's Cross train comes off the Victoria Bridge and curves towards Penshaw, on 7th September 1980. The practice of displaying HST formation numbers has since been discontinued, but some power cars display their number in the same place.
David H. Allen

Plate 69 (below left): A view of Penshaw North signal box the day after its closure, as the 13.08 (SuO) Heaton to Red Bank empties train passes by, on 25th April 1982. A panel installed in Usworth signal box now controls the section previously worked by Washington and Penshaw.
David H. Allen

Plate 70 (right): Almost eclipsed by a northbound HST, Class 55 'Deltic', No. 55018 *Ballymoss* approaches Leamside, on 8th March 1981, with the 11.25 (SuO) Edinburgh to Plymouth working.
David H. Allen

Plate 71 (below): Class 40, No. 40143 passes Washington, with the Red Bank empty vans train, on 18th April 1982. Later the same week, the signal box was closed, and the semaphore signals abolished.
David H. Allen

Consett

Plate 72: Class 31/1, No. 31319 propels its train of scrap out of the low yard at Consett, and on to a headshunt alongside the Blackhill branch, on 23rd December 1981. The signalling and the controlling signal box at Consett North are no longer operative.

David H. Allen

Plate 73 (above right): Complete with snowploughs at both ends, Class 31/1, No. 31215 moves from Carr House West signal box to the high yard at Consett, on 22nd December 1981, prior to returning to Tyne Yard.

David H. Allen

Plate 74 (below right): Only three months before the closure of the BSC Works at Consett, Class 37 locomotives, Nos. 37212 and 37141 climb past Anfield East, on 20th April 1980, with the 14.45 Redcar Ore Terminal to Consett Works train.

Les Abram

Plate 75: The signalman at South Pelaw gives the authority to the driver of Class 37, No. 37058 to enter the 'one train working' section to Consett, on 25th October 1982. South Pelaw signal box has since been demolished, and the 'one train working' section has been extended to Tyne Yard. Since 5th June 1983, the branch has been worked by just one line for both directions.

David H. Allen

Plate 76: This view of the low yard, on 25th October 1982, shows the extent of the destruction at Consett. Before the closure of the works, this yard was used to despatch the finished products. Making its second visit of the day, Class 37, No. 37058 prepares to depart with scrap for Tyne Yard.

David H. Allen

Plate 79 (below right): Class 31/1, No. 31134 heads south past Ouston Junction, with a train of scrap derived from the demolition of Consett Steelworks, on 15th July 1983. The train had earlier been worked into Tyne Yard by a Class 37 locomotive.

David H. Allen

Plate 77: In addition to scrap, the only other traffic handled on the Consett branch is domestic coal. This is now concentrated in the high yard, but before its closure, on 7th June 1982, Blackhill was also a coal depot. In this view, captured on 10th February 1982, Class 31/1, No. 31290 shunts at the terminus, prior to returning to Tyne Yard.   *Les Abram*

Plate 78: The Royal visit by the Prince of Wales, on 3rd December 1982, produced two immaculate Class 31/4 locomotives, Nos. 31403 and 31415. Having already run round the train, the locomotives are ready to depart from Consett.   *Les Abram*

Coal Traffic

Plate 80: The recently-named Class 56, No. 56076 *Blyth Power* approaches Murton Crossing, on 9th February 1983, with a working from East Hetton Colliery to Blyth Power-Station.

David H. Allen

Plate 81 (above right): Class 37, No. 37073 approaches Pelaw, on 22nd March 1982, with a trip working from Tyne Yard to Wardley.

Paul D. Shannon

Plate 82 (below right): Class 31/1, No. 31263 approaches Bowesfield, on 20th March 1982, with a train of stockpiled Polish coal, travelling from Lackenby to Hartlepool.

Paul D. Shannon

Plate 83: Class 37, No. 37200 arrives at Ashington Colliery, on 28th October 1982, with empties from Blyth Power-Station. To the right is one of the ex-BR Class 15 locomotives, which are used extensively in the area by the NCB.

David H. Allen

Plate 84: The heat haze on 3rd June 1982 somewhat softens the outline of Horden Colliery, as Class 37, No. 37226 draws forward, prior to attaching the brake van and departing with an afternoon train for Lackenby.

David H. Allen

Plate 85: Class 37, No. 37031 draws out of Wearmouth Colliery, with loaded hoppers for Sunderland South Dock, on 2nd September 1982.

David H. Allen

Plate 86: On 28th July 1970, Class 37 locomotive, No. 6788, since renumbered 37088, complete with brake tender, propels loaded hoppers, which form a train from Wearmouth Colliery, off the Southwick branch. The goods yard on the right of the picture has since closed, and Monkwearmouth Station, seen between the signal posts, is now a railway museum.

Ian S. Carr

Plate 87: Class 56, No. 56080 comes off the Newburn branch at Scotswood, with a train of empties from Stella North Power-Station, on 14th May 1982. At the time, Newcastle to Carlisle passenger trains used the lines to the left. The signal box has now been closed.

Les Abram

Plate 88: Prior to forming a morning departure from Dawdon Colliery on 6th February 1982, Class 37, No. 37066 arrives at Seabanks with a brake van. The lines to the right lead down to Seaham Harbour.

David H. Allen

Viaducts . . .

Plate 89:   Class 47/4, No. 47408 crosses the River Wear at Croxdale, while heading the 15.18 Newcastle to Liverpool train, on 13th March 1982.

David H. Allen

Plate 90:   On a short diversion over the High Level Bridge, on 25th October 1981, Class 47/4, No. 47417 hauls the 11.25 (SuO) Edinburgh to Plymouth train, composed of 13 vehicles.

David H. Allen

Plate 91: With the Penshaw Monument on the skyline, the 10.00 King's Cross to Edinburgh train crosses the Victoria Bridge, on 18th April 1982. The telegraph poles contrast with the modern image of the HST.

David H. Allen

Plate 92: Class 47/4, No. 47430 heads the 10.30 King's Cross to Dundee relief train across Yarm Viaduct, on 5th July 1981. This massive structure is over half a mile long, and has 42 arches.

David H. Allen

Plate 93:   An unidentified Class 37 locomotive heads a northbound coal train over the viaduct at Langley Moor, on 6th June 1983.

David H. Allen

Plate 94:   Class 55 'Deltic', No. 55022 *Royal Scots Grey* crosses the Royal Border Bridge at Berwick-upon-Tweed, while heading the 09.00 King's Cross to Berwick service, on 28th April 1979. As a result of the Penmanshiel Tunnel collapse, many East Coast Main Line Anglo-Scottish expresses were terminated at Berwick. Passengers were then conveyed by coach to Dunbar, prior to recommencing their rail journey. Some trains were diverted via Carlisle, with passengers avoiding a change of transport mode.

David H. Allen

Plate 97:   Class 31/1, No. 31276 heads a Darlington to Tyne Yard trip working though Croxdale, on 10th August 1981.
David H. Allen

Plate 95 (above left):   Class 47/4, No. 47524 climbs the 1 in 120 gradient through Neville's Cross Cutting, with the 09.50 Newcastle to Poole train, on 10th February 1983.

David H. Allen

Plate 96 (below left):   Class 37, No. 37165 passes through Croxdale with the 22.38 (MThO) Grangemouth to Haverton Hill train, on 26th May 1981. This train conveys hydrocyanic acid, and barrier vehicles are being used at the front and rear of the wagons.

David H. Allen

Durham ~ Thro' the Years

Plate 98: Class 47/4, No. 47414 pauses at Durham, with the 19.05 (SuO) Newcastle to Liverpool train, on 14th June 1981. The Norman cathedral, which dominates the town, can be seen in the background.

David H. Allen

Plate 99: Durham Gilesgate retained freight traffic for over a century after the loss of passenger traffic. On 5th August 1966, a Clayton Class 17 locomotive shunts in the terminus, after arriving with the daily goods train from Tyne Yard. The station was closed the following November, but the buildings remain, and the impressive facade is illuminated at night.

Ian S. Carr

Plate 100: In the not too distant past, the Durham Miner's Gala was a very big event, and produced many extra trains. In this instance, on 20th July 1963, a green-liveried diesel multiple unit approaches the station from the north, with the 11.27 train from Usworth. The train would have joined the main line at Newton Hall Junction. The station layout and signalling have been radically altered since this picture was taken.

Ian S. Carr

Plate 101: On 17th May 1977, Class 47/3, No. 47356 approaches Stone Bridge, with a southbound evening Freightliner service. At this time, several of the class still boasted green liveries.

David H. Allen

Plate 102: Class 45/0 'Peak', No. 45055 *Royal Corps of Transport* approaches the site of Deerness Valley Junction signal box, while heading the Newcastle to Trafford Park Freightliner service, on 6th June 1983.

David H. Allen

Plate 103: Pictured when both locomotives were new, Class 29, No. D6138 hauls Class 40, No. D259 (since renumbered 40059) over Relly Mill Viaduct, on 12th February 1960. Today, there are no semaphore signals, no junctions and no signal box at this location. Even the locomotives have been withdrawn from service!

Ian S. Carr

Plate 104: Class 47/4, No. 47446 enters Neville's Cross Cutting, with the 09.40 Edinburgh to Plymouth train, on 27th October 1981. The following Monday, this service was taken over by HSTs.

David H. Allen

Plate 105: Class 40, No. D246 (later renumbered 40046) takes the Bishop Auckland line at Deerness Valley Junction, while heading a diverted 'up' express, circa 1960. The twelve coach train appears to be entirely composed of pre-nationalization stock.

Ian S. Carr

Weardale

Plate 106: Class 37, No. 37007 winds its way through the Wear Valley to the west of Frosterly, with the 18.30 Eastgate to Carlisle train, on 9th June 1983.

David H. Allen

Plate 107: An evening train for Saltburn leaves Bishop Auckland, on 25th June 1983. The passenger services now use the former 'up' Durham platform, whereas those lines in the foreground are the freight lines to Eastgate.

David H. Allen

Plate 108: The first passenger train to call at Stanhope for 30 years did so on 25th June 1983, when a charter train ran from Darlington. Prior to returning, the train was stabled in the station. The Class 101 diesel multiple unit was composed of the following cars; E53188, E59077, E53170, E53251 and E54307. A similar excursion was planned for 10th September 1983.

David H. Allen

Plate 109: On 24th May 1982, Class 37, No. 37192 leaves Eastgate Cement Works, with a loaded train.

Les Abram

Plate 110 (above left): Signalman Ernie Dinsdale exchanges tokens with the driver of Class 37, No. 37119, as it heads the 15.05 Tees Yard to Eastgate cement empties train through Wolsingham, on 9th June 1983. The signal box and passing loop were abolished the following weekend. There is now no passing place between Bishop Auckland and Eastgate.

David H. Allen

Plate 111 (below left): Class 37, No. 37192 passes through the former Eastgate Station with the 08.45 (MO) Tyne Yard to Eastgate empties train, on 24th May 1982. This train is the stock off the 22.18 (FO) Grangemouth to Eastgate train, which stables at Tyne Yard over the weekend.

Les Abram

Plate 112: Class 37, No. 37045 crosses the River Wear at Etherley, with the 12.59 (MWFO) Eastgate to Heaton train, on 23rd August 1982.

David H. Allen

Plate 113: On 7th December 1981, Class 37, No. 37161 passes the lower quadrant distant signal near Witton-le-Wear, with a train for Eastgate.

Les Abram

Sunday Diversions

Plate 114: Having been diverted off the East Coast Main Line at Ferryhill, Class 55 'Deltic', No. 55013 *The Black Watch* slowly recovers from a speed restriction as it passes Bishop Middleham, while heading the 11.25 (SuO) Edinburgh to Plymouth train, on 21st June 1981.

David H. Allen

Plate 115: Class 47/4, No. 47442 passes Redmarshal en route for Stockton, with the diverted 12.05 (SuO) Newcastle to Liverpool train, on 26th July 1981. The iron spikes on the bridge are a reminder that the LNER overhead electrification scheme, from Newport to Shildon, followed this route.

David H. Allen

Plate 116: Class 55 'Deltic', No. 55007 *Pinza* drifts into Stockton with the 11.25 (SuO) Edinburgh to Plymouth service, on 29th March 1981. Diverted trains currently stop at Eaglescliffe to make the Darlington connection.

David H. Allen

Plate 117: Having been diverted via Leamside on 20th June 1982, Class 45/1, No. 45137 *The Bedfordshire and Hertfordshire Regiment (T. A.)* heads the 14.05 (SuO) Newcastle to Poole train, past the derelict Washington South Junction signal box. The route to South Pelaw formerly diverged to the left of the locomotive.

David H. Allen

Plate 118: On 15th February 1981, the 'down' trackbed through the station was being prepared, while trains were diverted via the station avoiding lines. Cravens diesel multiple unit, comprising cars E56454 and E50386, forming the 09.20 Newcastle to Middlesbrough train, passes by as the work is carried out. The station avoiding lines are no longer being used, and all traffic now passes through the platform lines.

David H. Allen

Plate 119: Diversions along the coast route are comparatively rare. However, the combined result of a landslip on the main line, and long-term improvements on the Leamside route, meant that such diversions took place for a week in 1979. In this view, Class 47/4, No. 47521, on 1st April, passes East Bolden with the 16.40 (SuO) Newcastle to King's Cross train.

David H. Allen

Plate 120: Two HSTs meet at Earsdon Junction while being diverted via the former Blyth & Tyne network, on 29th November 1981. On the left is the 11.25 (SuO) Edinburgh to Plymouth service, waiting for the 09.35 (SuO) King's Cross to Edinburgh train to come off the single line section from Benton. The route directly ahead is the line to Percy Main, which has since been closed.

David H. Allen

Plate 121: On 22nd May 1983, engineering work on the Bensham Underpass necessitated the diversion of Tyne Valley services along the East Coast Main Line. Trains were sent to Low Fell Junction for reversal, before proceeding along to Allerdene Junction to rejoin the normal route. Having reversed at Low Fell, the 09.42 (SuO) Newcastle to Carlisle train continues on its way.

David H. Allen

Plate 122: The 10.00 Edinburgh to King's Cross train passes the site of Fence Houses Station, on 15th March 1981, led by power car No. 43089.

David H. Allen

Plate 123: Class 37, No. 37032 hauls a train of 30 loaded HBA wagons past the sidings at Wearmouth, on 2nd March 1982.

David H. Allen

Plate 124: One of the original Derby lightweight diesel multiple units approaches Pontop Crossing, with a Leeds to Newcastle train, circa 1960. The formation is in original condition, with a front end chevron and green livery.

Ian S. Carr

Plate 125: The 12.27 Newcastle to Middlesbrough train approaches Hartlepool, on 3rd April 1982. All regular through passenger services use the 'down' platform, and the train can be seen crossing over to the 'down' line at Clarence Road signal box.
David H. Allen

Plate 126: On 14th November 1981, Class 31/1, No. 31163 heads the 12.56 'Footex' Sunderland to Middlesbrough train past Dawdon.

David H. Allen

Plate 127: 'Clayton' class diesel locomotive, No. D8593 comes off the South Dock branch at Ryhope Grange, on 29th April 1967. The train is being 'called on' into the run-round loop, prior to departing for the north. The gantry has since been demolished, and the Londonderry route in the foreground has been lifted.

Ian S. Carr

Shunter Duties

Plate 128: Class 03 shunter, No. 03022 shunts at Blaydon, after arriving with a trip working from Tyne Yard, on 26th October 1982. One month later, this locomotive was withdrawn from service.

David H. Allen

Plate 129: The Silksworth branch is now just a memory. Heading a loaded train from Silksworth Colliery to South Dock, on 31st July 1969, are two Class 03 shunters, Nos. D2053 and D2052.

Ian S. Carr

Plate 130: On 26th May 1980, Class 03 shunters, Nos. 03107 and 03066, stand at the western end of Newcastle Central Station.

David H. Allen

Plate 131:   Class 08 shunter, No. 08127 works in the low yard at Consett on 19th December 1979, only nine months before the complete closure of the steelworks.

David H. Allen

Plate 132:   On 28th July 1981, Class 08 shunter, No. 08232 propels two bogie-bolsters over the hump in Tees Yard.
David H. Allen

Plate 133: On 23rd August 1982, Class 08 shunter, No. 08063 shunts across Masons Arms Crossing at the BREL Shildon Works.
David H. Allen

Visitors

Plate 134: Replacing the usual Class 40 locomotive, Class 25/1, No. 25144 passes Bishop Middleham, on 17th May 1981, with the diverted 13.08 (SuO) Heaton to Red Bank train.

David H. Allen

Plate 135: On Wednesday 24th July 1963, a derailment at Ferryhill resulted in the diversion of East Coast Main Line services via Bishop Auckland. Having almost completed the diversion, the Class 50 prototype locomotive, No. DP2, heads the 10.10 King's Cross to Edinburgh train past Deerness Valley Junction.

Ian S. Carr

Plate 136: Having arrived in connection with the Rugby Union County Championship Final, a Western Region eight car diesel Pullman set stands at Hartlepool Station, on 13th March 1965.

Ian S. Carr

Plate 137 (below): No. D5702, a 'Metrovick' Co-Bo Type 2 diesel-electric locomotive heads a 13 coach test train through East Bolden, on 16th September 1958. Note the excellent condition of the wooden station nameboard.

Ian S. Carr

Plate 138: On 2nd July 1983, HST power car No. 43153 was named *University of Durham,* at Durham Station. Having arrived empty from Heaton, the power car was prepared for the unveiling at the end of the 'up' platform.

David H. Allen

Plate 139: The unveiling was carried out by the Chancellor of the University of Durham, Dame Margot Fonteyn de Arias. To her left is Mr F. Paterson, the General Manager of the Eastern Region. The model HST was presented to the Dame as a memento of the occasion.

David H. Allen

Naming Ceremony

Plate 140: Immediately after the naming ceremony, the HST set went into revenue-earning service by forming a special to Leeds. This set normally works empty coaching stock from Heaton to Leeds (Neville Hill).

David H. Allen

Plate 141: On 15th November 1981, Class 56, No. 56027 stands alongside Class 55 'Deltic', No. 55008 *The Green Howards* outside Gateshead Depot. The Class 56 locomotive was on loan for driver training, pending the arrival of an allocation of the class. The 'Deltics', on the other hand, had only a month left in revenue-earning service.
David H. Allen

Plate 142: A typical assemblage of motive power, viewed at the east end of Gateshead Depot, on 12th June 1983.

David H. Allen

Plate 143: Class 37, No. 37216 passes Relly Mill, on 31st August 1982, with the 09.15 Haverton Hill to Leith or Grangemouth service.

David H. Allen

Company Trains

Plate 144: Class 08 shunter, No. 08888 is pictured during the unloading of cement, on 25th July 1983, at the Ribble Cement Terminal at Railway Street, Newcastle. Once unloaded, the empties will form the 13.30 (TO) train for Clitheroe. The route in the foreground is the former Carlisle main line, but is now only used to reach several industrial users.

David H. Allen

Plate 145 (below): Class 37, No. 37045 prepares to leave Thrislington, on 30th March 1983, with a train of air-braked stock.

David H. Allen

Plate 146: With the Boulby Mine in the background, Class 47/0, No. 47226 approaches Grinkle Tunnel with a mid-afternoon train for Teesport, on 26th February 1982.

David H. Allen

Plate 147: Nature appears to be taking over on the Norton east to west curve, as Class 37, No. 37078 hauls a Thrislington to Cemetery North train, on 23rd July 1983. This short route is rumoured for early closure, with existing services being re-routed via Darlington.

David H. Allen

Cleveland

Plate 148: The grandeur of Saltburn Station has somewhat been compromised by the era of the paytrain diesel multiple unit and the bus stop style of platform shelter. A large part of the station has been demolished to make way for non-railway developments. The train is the 15.52 service for Bishop Auckland, and is seen on 1st June 1983.

David H. Allen

Plate 149: An afternoon Saltburn to Bishop Auckland train, on 1st June 1983, approaches Redcar Central.

David H. Allen

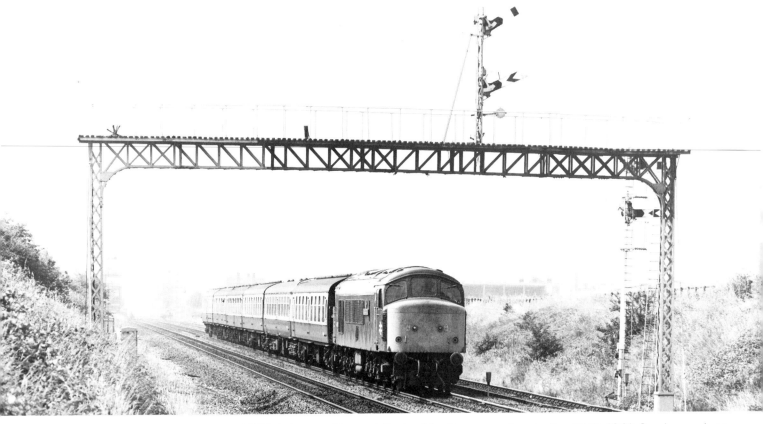

Plate 150: Class 46 'Peak', No. 46026 *Leicestershire and Derbyshire Yeomanry* heads the 10.35 (SO) Scarborough to Newcastle train through Norton, on 23rd July 1983. This is now the only regular locomotive-hauled passenger train using the coast route. The locomotive had recently been repainted at Gateshead Depot.

David H. Allen

Plate 151: Class 40, No. 40143 reaches the top of the 1 in 44 gradient at Nunthorpe, as it heads a day excursion from Leicester to Whitby, on 6th September 1981. The signalman is waiting with the single line token, to allow the train to proceed to Battersby.

David H. Allen

Plate 152: Class 47/0, No. 47226 heads a morning working from Boulby to Teesport, on 26th February 1982, past Crag Hall signal box. The sidings to the left serve the BSC Works at Skinningrove.

David H. Allen

Plate 153: To gain access to the large potash mine at Boulby, a section of the old Middlesbrough to Whitby coast route had to be relaid. On 26th February 1982, Class 37, No. 37172 heads a train of empties for Boulby, over the newly-built viaduct which traverses the A174 road at Carlin How.

David H. Allen

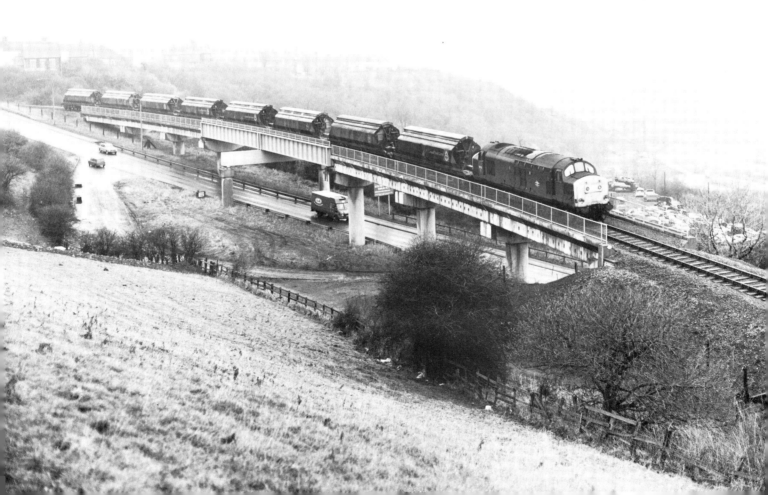

Speedlink

Plate 156 (above): Class 47/0, No. 47198 passes Newton Hall with the 16.18 (FO) Dover Town to Tyne Yard Speedlink train, on 2nd July 1983. It is now over ten years since the course of the East Coast Main Line was re-routed, but the former trackbed is still very conspicuous, and is seen to the left of the train.

David H. Allen

Plate 154 (above left): The 16.05 Tyneside Central Freight Depot to Paddock Wood Speedlink service passes Browney, on 31st May 1983.

David H. Allen

Plate 155 (below left): Some two hours earlier, the train depicted above was being prepared by Class 03 shunter, No. 03094, at the Tyneside Central Freight Depot.

David H. Allen

Plate 157 (below): Class 31/1, No. 31101 passes Norton East with an air-braked service from Tees Yard to Haverton Hill, on 30th August 1983. The train is composed of one ICI (Mond Division) wagon and a barrier vehicle.

David H. Allen

Engineering Operations

Plate 158: The main line functions normally as Class 31/1, No. 31107 passes the activity at Ouston Junction, on 5th June 1983. The work involved the reduction of the Consett route to a single line, and the restoration of the connection between the 'down' fast and the 'down' slow lines.

David H. Allen

Plate 159: During the early summer of 1980, much of the South Hetton Colliery branch was relaid. Between movements, on 29th June 1980, Class 37, No. 37196 stands next to Seaton Bank Top. The 'down' track had already been laid, but not aligned. The whole of this route is now scheduled to be reduced to a single track.

David H. Allen

Plate 160: Class 37, No. 37067 stands, on 28th February 1982, at the head of a short ballast train near Shildon Station.

David H. Allen

Plate 161: The 'up' passenger track was being relaid at Thornaby, on 12th April 1981, as a Class 105 two car diesel multiple unit, composed of cars E56423 and E51489, passes on the 'up' freight lines with the 09.40 Middlesbrough to Newcastle train. Class 47/0, No. 47093 is stationary with a ballast train. Visible beneath the footbridge are the station buildings, which have since been demolished.

David H. Allen

Plate 162: On 8th December 1982, Class 37, No. 37100 heads a ballasting operation on the 'down' through line at Durham.

Craig Oliphant

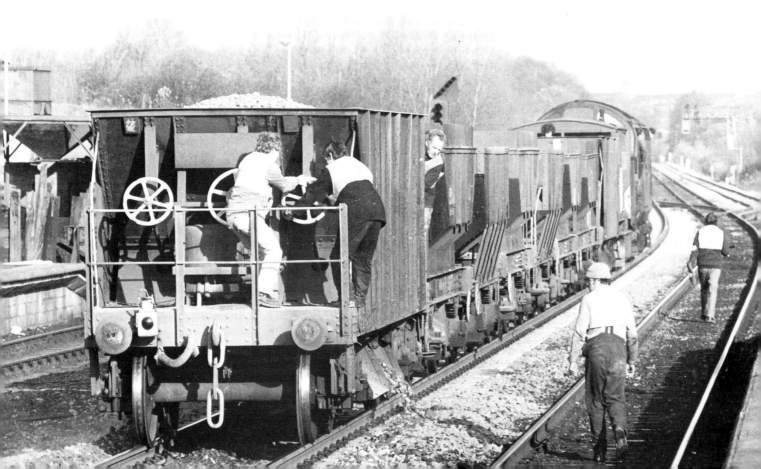

Plate 163:   Having just crossed over the East Coast Main Line, on 30th March 1983, Class 31/1, No. 31292 approaches South Pelaw with track which has been reclaimed from the closed route between Washington South Junction and South Pelaw.

David H. Allen

Plate 164:   Prior to running down to Tyne Yard, Class 47/0, No. 47013 stands at South Pelaw with redundant track, on 6th April 1983. There is no evidence of the large signal box that once controlled the junction.

Les Abram

Plate 167 (above right):   Class 55 'Deltic', No. 55011 *The Royal Northumberland Fusiliers* drifts into Alnmouth Station, on 11th October 1980, while heading the 13.20 Newcastle to Edinburgh train.

David H. Allen

Rural Northumberland

Plate 165:   Having just crossed the River Wansbeck, on 26th October 1981, Class 47/0, No. 47137 slows for the Morpeth stop while heading the 07.18 Edinburgh to Carlisle train.

David H. Allen

Plate 166:   An HST speeds south near Longhoughton, on 11th October 1980, with an afternoon Anglo Scottish service.

David H. Allen

Plate 168:   Class 55 'Deltic', No. 55006 *The Fife & Forfar Yeomanry* speeds through Widdrington with the 07.25 Plymouth to Edinburgh train, on 29th March 1980. The signal box was closed soon afterwards. The closed-circuit television masts were already in place.

David H. Allen

Freightliner Services

Plate 169: Recently overhauled Class 37, No. 37109, has difficulty in gaining adhesion, as it starts a heavily-loaded Freightliner service for Darlington out of the Stockton Terminal, on 31st May 1983.

David H. Allen

Plate 170: Class 47/0, No. 47211 leaves the Stockton Freightliner Depot, with an evening departure, on 31st May 1983. The terminal is constructed at the end of the remains of the Beck branch.

David H. Allen

Plate 171: An unidentified Class 37 locomotive heads a rather lightweight 18.05 Stockton to Darlington Freightliner service through Hartburn, on 7th June 1983.

David H. Allen

Plate 172: Two 'Peaks' meet at King Edward Bridge Junction, on 15th July 1983. Class 46, No. 46037 heads the Freightliner service for Trafford Park, while Class 45/1, No. 45118 prepares to cross the River Tyne with the 14.05 Liverpool to Newcastle train. Since the photograph was taken, the four tracks from Gateshead have been reduced to two, and the junction layout has been simplified.

David H. Allen

Plate 173: On 30th July 1981, Class 37, No. 37083 heads a 'down' coal train through Heaton.

David H. Allen

Plate 174: Class 37, No. 37200 passes Green Lane with a trip working from Dean Road sidings to Seaham, on 22nd December 1982. The train is passing the site of the former Tyne Dock Steam Shed.

David H. Allen

Plate 175: On 20th March 1982, a rather grimy Class 37, No. 37216, enters Cliff House sidings at Hartlepool, with a train of empty hoppers from the north.

David H. Allen

Plate 176: Class 37, No. 37200 leaves the NCB exchange sidings at Isabella, on 15th August 1983, with empty hoppers for Bedlington.

David H. Allen

Plate 177: A Class 37 locomotive negotiates the Kelloe Bank Foot branch with a coal train from East Hetton Colliery, on 26th August 1980. The colliery has since been closed, and the only traffic on the branch now originates from the Raisby Quarry.

David H. Allen

Plate 178: Class 37, No. 37066 heads the 11.30 Carlisle Yard to Tyne Yard mixed freight train past Blaydon, on 25th July 1983. The locomotive is passing the former junction with the direct route to Newcastle via Scotswood, which closed in 1982.

David H. Allen

Plate 179: A Heworth-bound Metro service runs neck and neck with the 12.15 Newcastle to Middlesbrough train, as it approaches Felling. The first British Rail station on leaving Newcastle is now Heworth.

David H. Allen

Plate 180: To gain access to ICI Callerton & Rowntrees at Fawdon, British Rail have been granted running powers over the Metro route to Bank Foot. A derailment on 5th July 1983 resulted in the Metro services being withdrawn for the best part of a day. The breakdown train is seen near Bank Foot Station, headed by Class 37, No. 37146 and Class 31/1, No. 31178.

David H. Allen

Plate 183 (above right):   Class 37, No. 37109 passes Hebburn with the 12.15 Jarrow (Shell) to Grangemouth empty tank train, on 29th July 1983. On the right is the unopened Metro route from Heworth to South Shields. The British Rail freight line and the Metro route run parallel, both being single lines with passing loops.

David H. Allen

Plate 181:   Green-liveried Class 40, No. D252 (since renumbered 40052) enters Whitley Bay with an excursion from Burton-on-Trent, on 20th August 1972. The train travelled via the south-east curve at Benton, before proceeding empty to Heaton via Wallsend. British Rail no longer has any access to this route.

Ian S. Carr

Plate 182:   Heaton Station was closed completely when the service to Tynemouth was withdrawn. A 'Peak' class locomotive passes through the station with empty stock for Heaton carriage sidings, before the buildings and platforms were razed to the ground.

Ian S. Carr

Plate 184 (below right):   Class 37, No. 37199 passes Jarrow Station, while heading the 12.20 Teesport to Jarrow (Shell) train, on 29th July 1983. The Metro station is built on the site of the former British Rail structure, and appears to be complete.

David H. Allen

On Test

Plate 185: Fresh from overhaul and resplendent in its new livery, Class 50, No. 50010 *Monarch* heads the Doncaster test train along the Darlington avoiding line, on 26th May 1981. The stock, now used on this train, comprise departmental Mk. I coaches.

David H. Allen

Plate 186: Class 31/1, No. 31301 heads a rather interesting combination of rolling stock past Ouston Junction, on 15th July 1983. In addition to the various research vehicles are three cars of a Class 317 electric multiple unit. It is seen on the outward leg of a York - Newcastle - York working.

David H. Allen

Plate 187:   Class 50, No. 50031 *Hood* approaches Plawsworth with a test train, on 31st May 1978. The locomotive, although having been allocated a name was not, however, carrying a nameplate.

David H. Allen

Plate 188:   Class 56, No. 56024 runs light through Neville's Cross Cutting, on 3rd September 1981. It has just emerged from Doncaster Works, after undergoing a light overhaul.

David H. Allen

Plate 189:   Class 50, No. 50027 *Lion* heads southward near Sunderland Bridge, with the Doncaster test train on 28th July 1983.

David H. Allen

Plate 192: Class 55 'Deltic', No. 55021 *Argyll & Sutherland Highlander* stands at Darlington Station on 30th December 1981, with the 20.25 Edinburgh to King's Cross service.

David H. Allen

Plate 190 (above left): Night just begins to fall as Class 31/1, No. 31275 pauses at Durham, while heading the 14.10 King's Cross to Edinburgh 'Premium Parcels' service.

Craig Oliphant

Plate 191 (below left): The driver looks on as Class 55 'Deltic', No. 55006 *The Fife & Forfar Yeomanry* waits to re-start the 20.43 Berwick to York train, on 11th May 1979.

David H. Allen

Plate 193: Class 46, No. 46011 arrives at Darlington on 30th December 1981 with the 21.10 departure from Newcastle, which ran via the coast. This portion was then attached to the 20.25 service from Edinburgh to King's Cross which ran without sleeping cars until January 1982, and was finally discontinued on 2nd October 1982.

David H. Allen

Memorabilia

Plate 194: *Wilton Endeavour* is the only named locomotive allocated to Thornaby Depot. The naming ceremony of Class 47/3, No. 47361 took place at Wilton, on 22nd July 1983.

Plate 195: Class 47/4, No. 47401 was the first ever Class 47 locomotive to be built. The original British Railways Number, 1500, can be seen underneath the present one.

Plate 196: This photograph shows the nameplate which is attached to Class 46 'Peak', No. 46026. In common with all other surviving Class 46 'Peaks', this one is allocated to Gateshead.

Plate 197: Class 55 'Deltic', No. 55011 *The Royal Northumberland Fusiliers* spent almost all its life at Gateshead. In the last operative years of the class, all survivors went to York Depot.

City of Newcastle upon Tyne

Plate 198: The first HST power car to be named was the Heaton-based No. 43113, with the naming ceremony taking place at Newcastle Station on 26th April 1983.

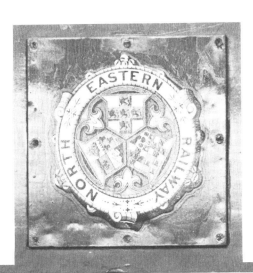

Plate 199: Class 47/4, No. 47401 was named *North Eastern* at Gateshead Depot, on 18th December 1981. Six of Gateshead's Class 47/4 locomotives have been similarly treated.

North Eastern

Shildon County Durham

SHILDON RAILWAY WORKS
150 YEARS
1833 – 1963

Plate 200: The naming of HST power car, No. 43078 after the BREL Wagon Works is an acknowledgement of the long association of Shildon with the railways. It is unfortunate that the naming can also be seen as an epitaph, as the future of the works is in grave doubt.

'Deltic' Finale

Plate 201: The green-liveried Class 55 'Deltic', No. 55002 *The King's Own Yorkshire Light Infantry* heads 'The Celtic Deltic' north of Tursdale Junction, on 31st October 1981. This was one of several BR sponsored specials, commemorating the imminent demise of the 'Deltics'.

David H. Allen

Plate 202: On 7th November 1981, BR organized another Anglo-Scottish 'Deltic' trip. It is seen during a brief pause at Hartlepool, being hauled by Class 55 'Deltic', No. 55015 *Tulyar*. The train ran from King's Cross to Edinburgh, via Leeds. Supposedly, because it followed the former course of the 'Queen of Scots Pullman', the train carried 'The Deltic Queen of Scots' headboard. However, instead of working through Harrogate, it followed the Durham Coast.

David H. Allen

Plate 203: The bright marker lights emphasize the gloom as a grimy Class 55 'Deltic', No. 55017 *The Durham Light Infantry* pauses at Durham Station, with the 05.50 King's Cross to Aberdeen train. This was the penultimate occasion on which the train was hauled by a member of the class.

David H. Allen

Plate 204: A very sad occasion as Class 55 'Deltic' No. 55022 *Royal Scots Grey* makes its last northbound revenue-earning trip along the East Coast Main Line, with the 05.50 King's Cross to Aberdeen train, on 31st December 1981. It is seen at Durham, just as the morning mist was being penetrated by the weak winter sun. The locomotive was on its way to Haymarket Depot, prior to working the southbound 'Deltic Farewell' on the following Saturday.

David H. Allen

Plate 205: Class 55 'Deltic', No. 55009 *Alycidon* approaches Hexham Station on 28th November 1981, with another of the 'Farewell to the Deltic' trips. This was an excursion from Newcastle to Edinburgh, the outward trip journeying via Carlisle and the homeward trip running along the East Coast Main Line.

David H. Allen

Plate 206: A typical October morning is disturbed by Class 55 'Deltic', No. 55022 *Royal Scots Grey* as it heads the 05.50 King's Cross to Aberdeen service, on 24th October 1981. The locomotive had recently acquired a copy of it's original number, D9000. This view is at Newton Hall, on the deviation which was opened to traffic in 1970.

David H. Allen